Colorado Tribune Publishing Company

Colorado Stock Laws

Colorado Tribune Publishing Company

Colorado Stock Laws

ISBN/EAN: 9783743313231

Manufactured in Europe, USA, Canada, Australia, Japa

Cover: Foto ©ninafisch / pixelio.de

Manufactured and distributed by brebook publishing software
(www.brebook.com)

Colorado Tribune Publishing Company

Colorado Stock Laws

COLORADO

STOCK LAWS.

COMPILED AND COLLATED

IN PURSUANCE OF THE PROVISIONS OF

"AN ACT TO PROVIDE FOR THE COMPILATION
AND COLLATION, PRINTING AND DIS-
TRIBUTION OF ALL ACTS AND
PARTS OF ACTS RELAT-
ING TO STOCK."

APPROVED FEB. 12, 1883.

DENVER, COLO.:
TRIBUNE PUBLISHING COMPANY.
1883.

OFFICERS OF THE COLORADO CATTLE GROWERS' ASSOCIATION.

JACOB SCHERRER . . . . *President.*
J. F. BROWN . . . . *Vice-President.*
L. R. TUCKER . . . . *Secretary.*
J. A. COOPER . . . . *Treasurer.*

EXECUTIVE COMMITTEE:

R. G. WEBSTER,   W. H. H. CRANMER,
    JOSEPH W. BOWLES,   H. H. METCALF,
           J. W. SNYDER.

Office: Rooms 4 and 5 Opera House Block, Denver, Colorado.

STATE INSPECTION COMMISSIONERS:

J. W. PROWERS . . . . of Bent County. .
J. L. BRUSH . . . . of Weld County.
NELSON HALLOCK . . . . of Lake County.
L. R. TUCKER . . . . of Elbert County.
GEORGE W. THOMSON, JR. . of Fort Lewis, La Plata County.

The following comprises all the General and Special Laws relating to Domestic Animals in the State of Colorado:

AN ACT TO AMEND AN ACT ENTITLED "AN ACT REGULATING THE BRANDING, HERDING AND CARE OF STOCK," CHAPTER TWENTY-SIX OF THE GENERAL LAWS.

[See Laws 1881, page 228.]

SECTION 1.   No person shall take up an estray animal, except in the county where he resides, and is a house-holder, nor unless the same be found in the vicinity of his residence.

Duties of persons taking up an estray.

When any person shall take up an estray, he or she shall, within five days after taking up such estray, make out a written description of such animal, or animals, as the case may be, setting forth all marks or brands apparent and other marks of identity, such as color, age, or size, and present the same to the County Clerk of the proper county, who shall endorse thereon the date of presentation of the same, and return one copy to the taker-up, and the copy he shall place upon record in the estray book.   After filing such notice, it shall be lawful for said taker-up to herd and take charge of said stock until the same shall be claimed and proved, and taken in charge by the owner thereof, or his duly authorized agent.   The County Clerk shall be entitled to twenty-five cents, from the party presenting the same, for recording each certificate of estray, and five cents per head for each additional number more than one contained in said certificate ; and the taker-up of said estray shall be entitled to twenty-five cents for each original certificate of description, with ten cents per head for each additional number more than one contained in said certificate, and mileage to and from the Clerk's office, at the rate of ten cents per mile; *provided,* That if the animal so taken up is a horse, mare, mule or colt, it shall not be lawful for the taker-up to so take charge of the animal or animals as hereinbefore provided, except to have the said animal or

Fees of County Clerk.

Pay of taker-up.

animals appraised by two householders, who shall be sworn before a justice of the peace, or any person qualified to administer oaths; said appraisers to receive one dollar and fifty cents each for services as such, said fees to be paid by the taker-up; said appraisement to be entered on the estray book at the same time and as part of the original description as aforesaid; *provided, further,* that it shall not be lawful for the taker-up of an animal or animals to so take charge of them as hereinbefore provided, except he or they cause to be published, within forty days of the time of such taking-up, a copy of the original notice as entered upon the estray book; such publication to be for four consecutive weeks; all estray notices to be published in the same paper for the current year; said paper to be located at the Capital, and to be designated by the State Stock Association, or in lieu thereof, by the Secretary of State. In the event of a change being made in the paper so selected, thirty days notice shall be given by the paper then publishing said notices. All expenses of said publication shall be paid by the taker-up, and by him collected, the same as other costs and charges, as hereinafter provided.

Approved February 11, 1881.

NOTE.—The provisions of sections 2, 3, 4 and 5, page 177, Session Laws of 1872, was in force until the session of 1881, when it was re-enacted.

[R. S., Chapter XCVI, page 847.]

SEC. 2. Before the owner of any estray so taken up and posted, shall be entitled to the possession of the same, he shall notify the taker-up of the time and place before the most convenient magistrate, county judge or justice of the peace, as the case may be, when and where he will prove his right to said property, and shall procure an order in writing from said magistrate to the taker-up to deliver the same over into the possession of the owner, upon payment to said taker-up of all the costs in the case, including the costs of taking up and ranching the said stock, at the rate of fifty cents per head per month; *provided,* that where the taker-up is fully satisfied that said estray or estrays are

Marginal notes: Pay of appraisers. Publication of estray notice. Expense of publication, how paid. In what manner owner of estray to recover possession.

the property of the claimant, and that he is entitled to the possession of the same, he may, upon payment to him of his legal costs and charges, deliver the same to the claimant, and take his receipt therefor for the stock so delivered; but the taker-up shall be held liable for the value of said stock, if he shall deliver the same to any one not the owner or entitled to the same. At the expiration of twelve months from the date of filing description of any estrays, and before the taker-up or other person not the rightful owner thereof, shall gain any title to said estrays, it shall be the duty of the taker-up to file a notice with the County Clerk, which shall be placed upon record in the estray book, setting forth a minute description of the estray to be offered; and the time and place when and where the same will be offered at public sale to the highest bidder, for cash in hand, and shall put up a copy of the same at the Court House door and in three other conspicuous places in the county, and one at the residence of the taker-up; said notice to be posted up for ten days before the day of sale.

Delivery of possession without proof of ownership before magistrate; liability of taker-up in such case.

Manner of making public sale of estray stock.

The sale shall be at public auction, to the highest bidder for cash in hand, and the proceeds of the same, after deducting all legal costs, fees and charges, shall be paid into the hands of the County Treasurer, for the benefit and use of the school fund of the school district in which the said estray stock was taken up. If the said district shall not be organized, then the same shall be paid into the general school fund of the county; *provided*, that no one shall have the right, for twelve months after the appearance of said stock, to advertise any animal which is branded with a brand recorded in the county where the animal is running.

Disposition of proceeds of sale.

Any Justice of the Peace of the county who is duly satisfied that the provisions of this act have been complied with by the taker-up, in all substantial parts, may, by order under his hand and seal, authorize the sale to be conducted by any constable or disinterested householder of the county, who shall execute and deliver to the purchaser a bill of sale of said stock, setting forth a description of the

Bill of sale by person conducting sale to vest good title in purchaser.

same and the price paid, and that the same was estray stock, which certificate shall vest a good and perfect title in the purchaser.

SEC. 3. If any person shall conceal, or attempt to conceal, any estray or lost goods, found or taken up by such person, or shall efface or change, or attempt to efface or change any mark or brand thereon, or carry the same beyond the limits of the county where found, or knowingly permit the same to be done, or shall neglect to notify, or give information of estray animals to the County Clerk of his county, every such person so offending shall be deemed guilty of larceny, and may be fined in any sum, at the discretion of the Court.

SEC. 4. No mustang or other inferior stallion over the age of one year; nor any Texan, Mexican, or Cherokee bull, or other inferior bull over the age of one year; nor any Mexican or other inferior ram over the age of two months, shall be permitted to run at large in this State; and no stallion of any kind over the age of one year shall be permitted to run at large in Boulder and Weld counties; nor shall any stallion over the age of one year be permitted to run at large in said State, except with a band of mares not less than ten in number. The owner or person in charge of such animal or animals as are prohibited from running at large by this section, who shall permit such animal or animals to run at large, may be fined for each offense not less than fifty dollars nor more than two hundred dollars. And it shall be lawful for any stock grower to castrate or cause to be castrated any such animal found running at large; *provided*, that if any person shall castrate any stallion, bull or ram, and it shall, on proper evidence before any competent court, be proven, to the satisfaction of said court, that such animal was not of a class of stock prohibited from running at large by this act, said person shall be liable to damages to the amount of treble the value of said animal so castrated, and costs of suit; *provided, also*, that for the purposes of this act, any stallion possess-

Marginal notes:

Punishment for concealment of estray or lost goods, effacing or changing, etc. mark or brand, neglecting to give information of estray animals.

Running at large of certain animals prohibited, penalty for permitting the same.

Castration of animals running at large, liability in case animal not prohibited.

ing one-quarter of mustang blood, shall be deemed a mustang stallion; any bull possessing one-quarter Texan, Mexican or Cherokee blood, shall be deemed a Texan, Mexican or Cherokee bull, as the case may be; and. any ram possessing one-quarter Mexican blood, shall be deemed a Mexican ram; and, *provided, further,* that this section shall not take effect and be in force within the counties of Huerfano, Las Animas, Costilla and Conejos.

(margin: What counties excepted.)

AMENDATORY TO AN ACT APPROVED FEBRUARY 9, 1872, RELATING TO STOCK INJURED OR KILLED BY RAILROAD OR RAILWAY COMPANIES.

[See R. S., page 850.]

SECTION 1. That an act entitled "An act providing for the payment for stock killed by railroads or railway companies," approved February 9, 1872, be and the same is hereby amended so as to read as follows:

SEC. 2. That every railroad or railway corporation or company operating any line of railroad or railway or any branch thereof, within the limits of this State, which shall kill, damage or kill any horse, mare, gelding, filly, jack, jenny or mule, or any cow, heifer, bull, ox, steer or calf, or any other domestic animal, by running any engine or engines, car or cars, over or against any such animal, shall be liable to the owner of such animal for the damages sustained by such owner by reason thereof.

(margin: Liability of railway corporation for damages to owner of animals killed or damaged.)

AMENDATORY TO CHAPTER NINETY-SIX, GENERAL LAWS.

[See Laws 1881, page 229.]

SEC. 2. [Sec. 3.] If the owner of any animal or animals so killed, or his or her authorized agent shall make affidavit before some officer authorized to administer oaths, that he or she was the owner or authorized agent of the owner of the recorded brand found upon the animal or animals so damaged or killed, at the time of such killing or damaging, and such person shall, within six months after

(margin: Affidavit of ownership and certificate of brand.)

2

such killing or damaging, deliver such affidavit to the agent or any officer of such company or corporation, together with a certificate of his or her mark or brand, under official seal of the County Clerk of the county in which such person resides, or shall make affidavit that the animal damaged or killed as aforesaid had no recorded mark or brand, and that he or she is the owner of such animal, [describing it] and the corporation or company shall pay to such person delivering such affidavit and certificate, or such affidavit last aforesaid, as follows:

SCHEDULE.

Schedule of payment.

Texas yearlings	$ 7 00
Texas two (2) years old	12 00
Texas three (3) years old and over	15 00
American yearlings	10 00
American two (2) years old	18 00
American three (3) years old and over	25 00
Amercan work cattle	25 00
American sheep, each	2 50
Mexican sheep or goats, each	1 50

All half-blood Texan, Mexican and American cattle shall be counted as Texas cattle, and all three-quarter [¾] blood American cattle shall be considered American cattle. Thoroughbred cattle, milch cows, high grade cows and grade bulls, shall be paid for at their cash value. Thoroughbred sheep shall be paid for at their cash value. Horses, mules and asses, shall be paid for at their cash value; *provided*, that no railroad company shall at any time be required to pay more than the market value of any animal killed or damaged. In all cases where such railroad company or corporation shall kill any of the stock mentioned in this act, and for which no price or sum is fixed, the owner or agent of such stock shall, after the filing of such affidavit and certificate of brand or affidavit of owner-

Selection of appraisers. ship as aforesaid, select some disinterested freeholder of the county where such killing took place, and shall notify such company or corporation of said selection, and such company or corporation shall within three days thereafter, select some suitable person to act with the person so selected, and the two so selected shall select a third, and the three so selected shall without delay proceed to appraise the value of the stock so killed, a majority of which three appraisers shall be sufficient to determine the same, and shall certify under oath such appraisement to an agent or superintendent of such company or corporation. In case such railroad or corporation shall refuse or neglect to appoint such appraisers, it shall be the duty of the Justice of the Peace nearest to the place where such stock is so killed, to select three disinterested persons as appraisers, and administer to them an oath to honestly appraise the value of such stock, which appraisers shall without delay appraise and forward to such justice the result of such appraisement, which justice shall within ten (10) days thereafter forward to an agent or superintendent of such railroad or corporation, a certificate of the result of such appraisement and the costs thereof; and such railroad or corporation shall, within thirty (30) days after the receipt of such certificate, pay to the owner of the stock so killed, or his or her agent, the amount of such appraisement together with all costs sa aforesaid ; and in all cases where the value of such stock is established by this act, such company or corporation shall pay for such stock within thirty (30) days after the delivery of the affidavit and certificate of ownership of brand or affidavit of ownership of stock. And all persons selected or appointed under this section, shall receive the sum of one dollar, to be paid by said railroad company or corporation as hereinbefore provided.

Approved February 11, 1881.

SEC. 4. Every railroad company shall keep a book, at some station in each county through which their road runs, to be designated by the company, and a notice of the station so designated shall be filed with the County Clerks of the counties in which such stations are located; and it is hereby made the duty of the said company to cause to be entered in said book, within fifteen days after the killing

Appraisement to be certified under oath.

Proceedure in case of neglect of R. R company to appoint appraiser.

Justice to forward certificate of appraisement to R. R. company.

When company to make payment.

Pay of appraisers.

Record of animals killed to be kept by railway corporation at some station in each county.

of any animal, a description as nearly as may be of such animal, its color, age, marks and brands, and shall keep said book subject to the inspection of persons claiming to have had animals killed. Should any company fail to keep said book, or to file such notice in the manner herein provided, or to enter therein such description of any animal killed for a period of fifteen days thereafter, such company shall be liable to the owner of such animal to an amount twice the full value thereof.

[AMENDATORY, SEE LAWS 1879, PAGE 188.]

SECTION 1. Any animal injured or killed not having any mark or brands upon it, or having marks or brands unknown to such company, by the trains of any railroad company, said company shall, within thirty days next after such injury or killing, pay the value thereof according to the schedule of prices now fixed by law, unto the Treasurer of the District Association of Cattle Growers within the district where such animal is thus injured or killed; *provided*, the ownership thereof shall not be established before the expiration of said thirty days; and, *provided*, *further*, that if there shall be no such association, then said money shall be paid into the treasury of the proper county to the credit of the school fund of the county.

Payment for stock killed without marks to whom made

SEC. 2. It shall be the duty of the Treasurer of such District Association to receive such money, and to receipt to such company therefor, and such receipt shall be a bar to any action that may be brought against such company on account of such injury for killing; and it shall be the further duty of such Treasurer to retain such money for six months, within which time he shall pay the same to the owner of such animal, in case the owner thereof shall be discovered; but in case the owner thereof shall not be discovered, then, and in that case, at the expiration of said six months, such money shall be deposited by such Treasurer to the credit of the general fund of such District Association.

Duty of district treasurer.

Sec. 5. [R. S.] If the owner of any stock shall drive any stock on the line of the track of any such company or corporation, with intent to injure such company or corporation, and such stock shall be killed or injured, such owner shall not receive any damage from such railroad company or corporation therefor, and shall be liable to such company or corporation for all damage such company or corporation may suffer in consequence of such act, and shall also be criminally guilty of a felony and liable to indictment therefor, and on conviction shall be imprisoned in the penitentiary not less than one nor more than five years; but nothing herein shall be construed to prevent any person from allowing his or her stock to pasture on the lands adjacent to the line of such railroads, or to drive his stock over or across any such track at suitable times and places. *Penalty for driving animals on line of railroad with intent to injure corporation; liability for damages to corporation.*

Sec. 6. In every case of the wounding or killing of any such cattle or sheep, the price of the damages for which is fixed by this act, the body of such animal shall belong to such company, unless the owner thereof shall elect to take the same in lieu of said damages, or part thereof, within twenty-four hours after said wounding or killing; but in every other case the railroad or railway company may proceed to take care of and preserve the body of said animal, and it shall be the duty of such company to preserve the hide of such animal for at least thirty (30) days after such killing, such hide or hides to be kept for thirty (30) days for inspection by said railroad company or corporation at the station house nearest to the place where such killing occurred. If any agent or employe of such company shall bury any animal killed or wounded by such company without skinning the same, or shall neglect to keep for thirty (30) days for inspection any hide so taken off as herein provided, such agent or employe of such company shall be fined in any sum not less than one hundred or more than three hundred dollars for each and every animal, to be collected in the name of the people of the State of Colorado, before any court of competent juris- *Disposition of body of animal killed or wounded. Penalty for burying animal without skinning and keeping the hide for inspection; disposition of fine.*

diction, one-half of the amount so received to go to the County Treasurer of the county wherein the recovery is had, and the other half to the person at whose instance the suit was brought.

Punishment for making false affidavit of ownership of animal killed.

SEC. 7. Any person falsely making an affidavit of ownership of any animal killed or damaged, shall, on conviction thereof, be liable to a fine of not less than five hundred dollars and imprisonment in the penitentiary for not less than one year.

AN ACT TO PROVIDE FOR THE BRANDING, HERDING AND CARE OF STOCK, AND TO REPEAL CERTAIN ACTS IN RELATION THERETO.

[See R. S., page 854.]

Punishment for driving animals from usual range. What proof requisite.

SECTION 1. Any person or persons not being the owner or owners, or having the right of possession of any animal or animals, who shall be found driving or leading any such animal or animals from its or their usual range, such person or persons may be arrested by any constable, officer, or other person, specially deputed for such purpose, by a judge or justice of the peace, and such person or persons may be taken before any court of competent jurisdiction for examination and trial, and if found guilty, shall be punished as for larceny. In prosecutions for a violation of the provisions of this section, it shall not be necessary, in order to warrant a conviction, for the people to prove that the offense was committed knowingly, or wilfully, or to show an intent, purpose or motive on the part of the accused; but if it shall be shown that the accused had in his possession, or under his control or supervision, any animal so being wrongfully led or driven from its usual range, as aforesaid, or that the accused assisted in so leading or driving away any such animal without having the right of possession thereof, as aforesaid, such showing shall be sufficient to warrant a conviction, unless the accused shall by testimony in his behalf explain the case made against him in such manner as to show good faith and an innocent purpose on his part.

SEC. 2.   Any dog found running, worrying or injuring sheep or cattle, may be killed, and the owner or harborer of such dog, shall be liable for all damages done by it. *Liability for damages done by dog.*

Section three reads as follows:

[See Laws 1881, page 236, section 23.]

SEC. 3.   Any person or persons owning or keeping any flock or herd of sheep, any portion of which flock or herd may be diseased with the scab, or with any other contagious disease to which sheep are subject, shall be liable in the full amount of damage that may be occasioned to other sheep owner or holder by reason of such diseased flock or herd of sheep, or any part thereof, being moved or allowed to stray from its own range while in such diseased condition. *Liability for damages caused by moving flock or herd of diseased sheep.*

SEC. 4.   Animals such as are usually branded, may be branded on either side with the owner's brand.   All brands shall be recorded in the county where the owners reside. No evidence of ownership by brands shall be permitted in any court in this State, unless the brands shall have been recorded as provided in this act.   Each drove of cattle or sheep which may be driven into or through any county of this State, shall be plainly branded or marked with one uniform brand or mark.   The cattle shall be so branded with the distinguishing ranch or road brand of the owner as to show distinctly in such place or places as the owner may adopt.   Sheep shall be marked distinctly with such mark or devise as may be sufficient to distinguish the same readily should they become intermixed with other flocks of sheep owned in the State; any such owner or owners, or person in charge of such drove, which may be driven into or through the State, who shall fail to comply with the provisions of this act, shall be fined not less than fifty (50) nor more than three hundred (300) dollars, at the discretion of the court. *Marks and brands not evidence unless recorded; manner of marking or branding droves of cattle or sheep driven into or through any county of this State; penalty for failure to comply with provisions of this act.*

Making and
recording of cer-
tificate of brand. SEC. 5. Any person desiring to use any brand, shall make and sign a certificate, setting forth a *fac simile* and description of the brand which he desires to use, and shall file the same for record in the office of the county clerk of the county wherein he resides, wh'ch clerk shall record the same in a book kept by him for that purpose, and from and after the filing of such certificate, the person filing the same shall have the exclusive right to use such brand within such county for the purpose aforesaid. And any person or persons so desiring may, in the manner and with **Record of sim-**
ilar marks or
brands ; penalty
for. like effect, as herein provided, record his brand or mark in any county in this State, into which his stock are liable to stray. *Provided,* that such mark or brand has not been heretofore recorded in such county by some other person, and if the clerk and recorder of any county shall for any persons record any mark or brand, there being at the time of such recording a similar living mark or brand upon the records of his county, such clerk and recorder shall be liable to pay a fine of not less than twenty (20) nor more than one hundred (100) dollars; *and provided further,* when two or more similar marks or brands have been heretofore recorded in any county, the oldest record shall entitle the owner to the exclusive use thereof in such county.

Punishment for
marking or
branding or de-
facing or obliter-
ating, etc., mark
or brand of ani-
mal the prop-
erty of another. SEC. 6. If any person shall brand or mark, or cause to be branded or marked, with his, her, or their brand, or any other not the recorded brand of the owner, any animal being the property of another, or shall efface, deface or obliterate any brand or mark upon any animal, any such person so offending shall be deemed guilty of larceny, and on conviction thereof, shall be confined in the penitentiary not less than one year, nor more than five, as the Court may direct, and shall also be liable to the owner thereof for three times the value of the animal so branded or marked, or upon which the brand or mark shall have been so effaced, defaced or obliterated, and in no case shall the payment of the forfeiture herein mentioned, entitle the person so branding, effacing, defacing or obliterating a brand

to the property in the animal so branded, or upon which the brand was effaced, defaced or obliterated, but such animall shall be surrendered to the proper owner.

Section seven reads as follows:

[See Laws 1879, page 189, section 3.]

SEC. 7. All neat stock found running at large in this State without a mother, and upon which there is neither ear mark nor brand, shall be deemed a mavorick, and may be taken in charge by the captain or foreman of a legal round-up, and sold at such time and places (place) and in such manner as shall be determined by the Executive Committee of the District Association of Cattle Growers of the district wherein such mavorick shall be taken up. The proceeds arising from such sales shall be paid unto the Treasurer of such District Association, and if any stock so sold shall, within the period of six months immediately following such sale, be claimed, identified and proven by the rightful owner, it shall be the duty of such Treasurer to forthwith pay the money received for such mavorick to such owner; but in the event that such mavorick shall not be thus identified and its ownership proven during said six months, then it shall be the duty of such Treasurer to carry the amount received therefor to the credit of the general fund of such association. The captain or foreman of a legal round-up who shall sell any stock under the provisions of this section, shall only sell the same for cash, and shall, within ten days after such sale, pay the proceeds thereof into such Treasurer. The person purchasing a mavorick at such sale, shall receive from such captain or foreman a bill of sale therefor, in his capacity of captain or foreman, describing the animal thus sold and showing the price paid therefor, which bill of sale shall convey unto such purchaser the title to such mavorick.

Approved February 12, 1879.

SEC. 8. Any captain or foreman of round-up who shall refuse or neglect to deliver to the County Treasurer all moneys received from the sale of "mavoricks" or unbranded stock sold by him, or who shall give a false or incorrect bill of sale of any stock sold, or shall refuse to give a bill of sale of any stock sold by him, shall be guilty of a misdemeanor, and on conviction thereof shall be fined or imprisoned, or both, at the discretion of the Court.

SEC. 9. Any person who shall mark or brand, or cause to be marked or branded, or in any way convert to his or her use, or allow the same to be done by his employe or agent in his behalf any animal known as a "mavorick," or any other animal not lawfully in possession of such person, except as otherwise provided in this act, shall be deemed guilty of larceny, and on conviction thereof shall be imprisoned not less than one month or more than one year, as the Court may determine.

Unlawful branding of mavoricks deemed larceny; how punished.

SEC. 10. Any stock grower of this State may adopt and use an ear mark, and such ear mark shall be taken in evidence in connection with the owner's recorded brand, in all suits at law or in equity in which the title to stock is involved. Such ear marks shall be made by cutting and shaping the ear or ears of the animal so marked, but in no case shall the person so marking an animal cut off more than one-half of the ear so marked ; neither shall any one mark by cutting an ear on both sides to a point. No County Clerk or Recorder shall record the same ear mark to more than one person.

Ear marks ; effect of in evidence ; same mark not to be recorded to more than one person.

SEC. 11. In all suits at law or in equity, or in any criminal proceedings, when the title to any stock is involved, the brand on an animal shall be *prima facie* evidence of the ownership of the person whose brand it may be ; *provided*, that such brand has been duly recorded as provided by law. Proof of the right of any person to use such brand, shall be made by a copy of the record of the same, certified to by the County Clerk of that county, or any county in which the same is recorded, under the hand and seal of office of such Clerk.

Recorded brand evidence of ownership in all suits ; how proof to be made

SEC. 12. When the stock of any resident shall intermix with any drove of animals, it shall be the duty of any drovers or persons in charge, to cut out and separate such stock from said drove immediately, except in case of sheep and horses, when they shall be driven to the nearest suitable corral to be separated. Any person, either owner or drover, or otherwise connected with the management of such drove, who shall neglect to comply with the provisions of this section, shall be fined in any sum not exceeding five hundred dollars ($500.00) for every offense, and shall be liable to indictment for larceny.

Duties of drovers in case stock of residents intermix with their herds or droves; penalty for failure or neglect.

SEC. 13. When the stock of any person in Colorado shall be driven off its range without the owner's consent, by the drover of any herd or drove, every person engaged as drover of such stock, or otherwise engaged in the care and management thereof, shall be liable to indictment and punishment as for larceny, and shall be liable for damages in the amount of two hundred dollars ($200.00) for each head so driven off, together with all costs accruing in the trial of said cause, and said herd of stock or a sufficient number to cover all damages and costs shall be held liable for the same.

Driving off stock from range deemed larceny; how punished.

SEC. 14. Any person owning or having charge of any drove of cattle, horses or sheep, who shall drive the same into or through any county of Colorado, of which the owner is not a resident or land owner, and where the land in such county is occupied and improved by settlers and ranchers, it shall be the duty of such owner or person in charge of such cattle, horses or sheep, to prevent the same from mixing with the cattle, horses or sheep, belonging to the actual settlers, and also to prevent said drove of cattle, horses or sheep, from trespassing on such land as may be the property or be in the possession of the actual settler and used by him for the grazing of animals or the growing of hay or other crops, or from doing injury to ditches. If any owner or person in charge of any said drove of stock shall wilfully injure any resident of the State by driving such drove of stock from the public highway, and herding the same on lands occupied and improved

Duties of owner or person having charge of drove passing through settled counties in preventing the same from mixing with cattle, horses or sheep, or trespassing on lands of settlers; penalty

by settlers in possession of the same, it shall constitute a misdemeanor, and shall be punished by a fine of not less than twenty-five or more than one hundred dollars, at the discretion of the Court, and render the owner or person in charge of the drove so trespassing liable for the damages done to such settler.

Penalty for trespass of hogs or swine running at large.

SEC. 15. No hog or swine shall be permitted to run at large, and the owner of any hog or swine trespassing on the property of any person shall be liable in treble the damages occasioned by such trespass, and a fine of not less than five nor more than ten ($10.00) for each offense.

Skinning of carcass of sheep or cattle without consent of owner; deemed and punished as larceny.

SEC. 17. Any person or persons who may skin or remove from the carcass any part of the skin, hide or pelt of any neat cattle or sheep found dead, without permission from the owner, shall be deemed guilty of larceny, and on conviction thereof shall be punished in the manner provided by law for the punishment of larceny ; *provided*, nothing herein shall be deemed to prevent the skinning of animals killed by railroad companies by the employes of any railroad company by which such stock may have been killed.

Cases in which bills of sale shall be given and received for stock sold or otherwise disposed of

SEC. 18. No person or persons, whether as principal or agent, shall hereafter sell or otherwise dispose of any neat stock, nor shall any person, whether as principal or agent, buy, purchase or otherwise receive any such stock, unless the person or persons so selling or disposing of any such stock shall give, and the person or persons buying, purchasing or otherwise receiving any such stock shall take a bill of sale in writing, of the stock so sold, or disposed of, or so bought, purchased or otherwise received, as the case may be, in any of the following cases, viz :

First—When such stock or any part thereof, is to be shipped from the State, or slaughtered by the purchaser, or when the said stock or any part thereof is to be, by any such purchaser, sold to any other person or persons for shipment or slaughtering, or is to be by any such other person or persons offered for sale for shipment or slaughtering."

Second—When any such stock is to be driven, led, taken or shipped to any market, range or other place more than ten miles distant from the place of delivery thereof, upon any such sale or purchase, or when any such stock is to be led, driven, taken or shipped to any market, range or other place more than ten miles distant from the place where such stock may be herded, or kept, or permitted to range at the time of the sale or purchase thereof, or to any market, range or other place more than ten miles distant from the place where such stock may have been herded, kept, or permitted to range, for any portion of the three months next preceding such sale or purchase."

Third—When any such stock so sold or purchased, is at the time of such sale or purchase, or for any part of the sixty days next prior thereto, has been running at large upon an unenclosed range; but this provision shall not apply to sales of stock where the persons who sell are selling stock of which they have had actual and personal control and supervision, daily, for the said period of sixty days next prior to the sale thereof, and are rightfully entitled either as principal or agent to sell and dispose of the same.

SEC. 19. Any person who shall violate or fail to comply with any of the provisions of the last foregoing section shall be deemed guilty of a misdemeanor, and upon conviction shall be fined in a sum of not less than twenty-five dollars nor more than five hundred dollars, or imprisoned in the county jail not less than thirty days, nor exceeding six months, or may be punished by both fine and imprisonment, in the discretion of the court. *Penalty for violation of preceding section.*

SEC. 20. It shall be the duty of any person who may have purchased or received, or have in his possession any such stock, either for himself or for another, to exhibit, on reasonable request to any person inquiring therefor, the bill of sale of such stock if in his power so to do, and if not in his power so to do, to state and give the reason therefor, and any person violating or failing to comply with the provisions of this section, shall be deemed guilty and liable to punishment as provided in the next preceding section. *Penalty for failure to exhibit bill of sale upon reasonable request.*

SEC. 21. The provisions of the last three sections shall be liberally construed in favor of the people, and, in order to convict of any offense made punishable in any of the said sections, it shall not be necessary for the prosecution to prove knowledge, intent, purpose or motive on the part of the accused, but such knowledge, intent, purpose and motive may be presumed where the wrongful act of the accused has been shown, and shall justify a conviction, unless the testimony in the case shall satisfactorily show the good faith and innocent purpose of the accused.

Liberal construction of three preceding sections; what proof necessary to conviction.

SEC. 22. Any person who shall steal, embezzle or knowingly kill, sell, drive, lead or ride away, or in any manner deprive the owner of the immediate possession of any neat cattle, horse, mule, sheep, goat, swine or ass, or any person who shall steal, embezzle or knowingly kill, sell, drive, lead or ride away, or in any manner apply to his own use any neat cattle, horse, mule, goat, sheep, ass or swine, the owner of which is unknown, or any person who shall knowingly purchase from any one not having the lawful right to sell and dispose of the same, any neat cattle, horse, mule, sheep, swine or ass, shall be deemed guilty of a felony, and on conviction thereof in any court of competent jurisdiction, shall be punished by imprisonment not exceeding six years, or by fine not exceeding five thousand (5,000) dollars, at the discretion of the court.

Punishment for stealing, killing, driving or leading away stock of another or of unknown owner, or purchasing from any one not having lawful right to dispose of such stock.

SEC. 23. All cases which are by this act declared to be larceny, and in all cases of felonious taking, stealing, riding, driving, leading and carrying away of any animal or animals herein referred to, the same shall be deemed, and taken to be, and the courts of this State shall construe the same to be grand larceny, subjecting the offender or offenders to be condemned to the penitentiary for a term of not less than one year nor more than ten years, except as otherwise provided for in this act, notwithstanding the value of such animal or animals may be less than twenty dollars.

What violation of this act construed to be grand larceny.

injured may take in custody such animals, and make complaint before the Justice of the Peace of the precinct in which such damage shall have been committed; whereupon such Justice shall proceed forthwith to appoint three disinterested appraisers, who shall appraise the damages caused, and report their decision to the Justice; and the party or parties whose stock shall have been found injuring any crops, as aforesaid, shall be held responsible for any and all damage so committed, to be collected in the same manner as in other cases, together with all costs of proceedings; and the animal or animals so found injuring any crops may be taken and held as a security for the payment of such damages and costs.

SEC. 3. The appraisers appointed under the provisions of the foregoing section shall be allowed the sum of twenty-five cents each, to be paid by the party whose animals shall have been found damaging. ^{Fee of appraisers.}

SEC. 4. That all acts and parts of acts incontistent with this act, be, and the same is hereby repealed.

. SEC. 5. This act shall take effect and be in force from and after its passage.

Approved February 12, 1881.

To amend an act to provide for the branding, herding and care of stock, and to repeal certain acts in relation thereto.

[See Laws of 1879, page 178, section 19.]

SECTION 19. The foreman of round-ups shall each receive three dollars per day for each day of actual service, and the Auditor shall draw his warrant therefor upon the presentation of a certificate signed by two or more of the proper Round-up Commissioners, and setting forth the number of days of service, the number of the district in which the labor was performed, and that such labor was performed at the spring round-up; and the Treasurer shall pay the same out of the round-up and inspection fund herein provided for; *provided*, that the aggregate wages of foreman in any one district shall in no case exceed one hundred and fifty dollars in any one year.

An Act to Amend an Act Entitled an Act to Pro-
vide for the Branding, Herding and Care of
Stock, and to Repeal Certain Acts in Relation
Thereto.

[Laws 1881, page 232, section 1.]

SECTION 1. The districts herein constituted shall be
called round-up districts, and their several limits shall be
as follows:

District No. 1.   SEC. 2.   District number one: Commencing at a
point where the State line crosses the Arkansas river,
thence up said stream to the mouth of the Purgatoire,
thence up the latter stream to Smith's Cañon, thence up
said cañon to its head, thence down Carrijo creek to the
State line, thence east to the southeast corner of the State,
thence north to the place of beginning.

District No. 2.   SEC. 3.   District number two: Commencing at the
mouth of the Purgatoire, thence up the Arkansas to the
mouth of the St. Charles, thence up the latter stream to the
east line of Custer county, thence south to the north line of
Huerfano county, thence westerly on said line to the west
boundary of the county, thence on said boundary to the
north boundary of Las Animas county, thence on the latter boundary to the Purgatoire, thence down said stream
to the place of beginning.

District No. 3.   SEC. 4.   District number three: Commencing at the
mouth of [the] St. Charles, thence up the Arkansas to Grape
creek, thence along the eastern slope of the Wet Mountains to the St. Charles, thence down said stream to the
place of beginning.

District No. 4.   SEC. 5.   District number four: Commencing at the
southeast corner of Custer county, thence along the southern and western boundary of said county to the boundary
of Fremont county, thence along the west boundary of the
latter county to the Arkansas river, thence down the Arkansas to Grape creek, then along the line of district number
three to the place of beginning.

Sᴇᴄ. 6.　District number five shall be limited by that District No. 5. part of Las Animas county lying west of the point where Carrijo creek crosses the southern boundary of the State.

Sᴇᴄ. 7.　District number six: Commencing where District No. 6. the east line of Pueblo county crosses the Arkansas, thence up said river to Cañon City, thence northerly along the base of the mountains to the north line of El Paso county, thence east on said line to the northeast corner of the county, thence south to place of beginning.

Sᴇᴄ. 8.　District number seven: Commencing at the District No. 7. northeast corner of El Paso county, thence south to the Arkansas, thence down said river to the east line of the State, thence north to the dividing ridge between the Republican and the Big Sandy, thence westerly along said ridge to Cedar Point, thence to River Bend, thence up Sandy to place of beginning.

Sᴇᴄ. 9.　District number eight: Commencing at District No. 8. River Bend, thence westerly on the line of the Kansas Division of the Union Pacific Railway to the Platte, thence up said stream to the mountains, thence southerly along the base of the mountains to the north line of El Paso county, thence east along said boundary to the head of the Sandy, thence down the Sandy to the place of beginning.

Sᴇᴄ. 10.　District number nine: Commencing on District No. 9. the Platte, at the mouth of Sand creek, thence down the former stream to the mouth of the Bijou, thence up the Bijou to Deer Trail, thence westerly along the line of the Kansas Division of the Union Pacific Railway to Sand creek, thence down said creek to place of beginning.

Sᴇᴄ. 11.　District number ten: Commencing at the District No 10. mouth of Bijou, thence up said creek to Deer Trail, thence on a direct line to Agate station, thence to Cedar Point, thence along the dividing ridge between the Republican and Big Sandy to the east line of the State, thence north on said line to the Platte, thence up said stream to the place of beginning.

District No. 11. — **SEC. 12.** District number eleven: Commencing at the mouth of Lodge Pole creek on the Platte, thence up the latter to the mouth of the Cache-la-Poudre, thence up the Cache-la-Poudre to the north line of the State, thence east on said line to the place of beginning.

District No. 12. **SEC. 13.** District number twelve: Commencing at the mouth of the Cache-la-Poudre, thence up the Platte to Brighten, thence along the line of the Boulder Valley Railway to Boulder City, thence along the base of the mountains to the Cache-la-Poudre, thence down said stream to the place of beginning.

District No 13. **SEC. 14.** District number thirteen: Commencing at Cañon City, thence along the easterly base of the mountains to the first correction line south, thence west on said line to the west line of Park county, thence on said line to the line of Fremont county, thence on the west line of said county to a point where it intersects with the Arkansas river, thence down said river to the place of beginning.

District No. 14. **SEC. 15.** District number fourteen shall be limited by the limits of Lake county.

District No 15. **SEC. 16.** District number fifteen shall comprise that part of the San Luis Valley lying north of the Rio Grande and the Denver & Rio Grande Railway.

District No. 16. **SEC. 17.** District number sixteen shall be bounded as follows: Commencing at Del Norte, thence down the Rio Grande to Alamosa, thence along the Denver & Rio Grande Railway to the east line of Costilla county, thence south on said line to the State line, thence west on said State line to the west line of Conejos county, thence north on said line to the north line of the county, thence to Del District No. 17. Norte on a direct line. District number seventeen shall be limited by the limits of La Plata county.

Round-up commissioners; appointment, qualification, powers **SEC. 18.** The Governor shall appoint three Commissioners for each district, on or before the first day of March of each year, to be known as Round-up Commissioners, and who shall be actual owners of cattle running upon the range within the district for which they are appointed.

Said Commissioners, or a majority of them, shall have power and may, on or before the first day of April of each year, arrange the programme for the annual spring round-ups, fix the time of their commencement, appoint a foreman, and remove the same for incompetency, neglect of duty, or other cause which by them shall be deemed sufficient.

SEC. 19. The Governor shall appoint, on or before the first day of May of each year, five Commissioners, from different sections of the State, to be known as the Board of Inspection Commissioners. No person who is not the actual owner of cattle upon the public range shall be eligible to serve on said board. Said Commissioners shall each take and subscribe to an oath conditioned upon the faithful performance of his duties as Commissioner, which oath shall be filed in the office of the Secretary of State. A majority of the board shall constitute a quorum to do business. *Inspection commissioners: appointment, qualification, oath, quorum.*

SEC. 20. It shall be the duty of said board to employ competent Cattle Inspectors, not exceeding eight in number, at any one time, and to distribute them at such points, either within or without the boundaries of the State, as will in their judgment, most effectually prevent the illegal slaughtering or shipping of cattle. They shall also furnish each Inspector with a list of all brands sent to them for that purpose and owned by residents of this State. All Inspectors while thus employed shall be subject to such reasonable rules and requirements as the board may prescribe, and shall be subject to dismissal by the board at any time. Said Inspectors shall each receive not to exceed the sum of one hundred dollars per month during their time of actual service, and the Auditor shall draw his warrant therefor, upon bills approved by the Board of Inspection Commissioners, and the Treasurer shall pay the same out of the inspection fund. *Duties of board of inspectors.*

SEC. 21. There shall be levied and assessed upon the assessed value of all taxable property in the State, in each *Levy.*

year, one-fifteenth of one mill on each and every dollar thereof, to be known as the inspector's tax, said tax to be assessed and collected in the same manner and at the same time as is now, or may be prescribed by law for the assessment and collection of State revenue.

County treasurer to keep separate fund.

SEC. 22. It shall be the duty of the County Treasurers of the several counties to preserve the fund thus provided for as a separate fund, and to transmit the same monthly to the State Treasurer, who shall keep the same in a fund to be known as the inspection fund.

Repeal.

SEC. 24. Section two thousand five hundred and ninety-two [2592] of the General Laws, and any other acts or parts of acts inconsistent herewith, are hereby repealed.

Approved February 8, 1881.

AN ACT TO SECURE TO RANCHMEN, TAVERN-KEEPERS AND OTHER PERSONS.

[Liens on Personal Property.]

Be it enacted by the General Assembly of the State of Colorado :

Lien given for care of stock, and retention of stock authorized

SECTION 1. That any ranchman, farmer, agistor or herder of cattle, tavern-keeper or livery-stable keeper, to whom any horses, mules, asses, cattle or sheep, shall be intrusted, for the purpose of feeding, herding, pasturing or herding, shall have a lien upon such horse, mules, asses, cattle or sheep, for the amount that may be due for such feeding, herding, pasturing or ranching, and shall be

Lien given to hotel and boarding house keepers on baggage, and its retention authorized.

authorized to retain possession of such horses, mules, asses, cattle or sheep, until the said amount be paid ; and every hotel, tavern, boarding-house keeper and every person who rents furnished rooms, shall have a lien upon the baggage of his or her patrons, boarders and guests, for such boarding, lodging or rent, or either, for the amount that may be due from such patrons, boarders, guests, tenants, for boarding, lodging or rent or either, and they are hereby authorized to hold and retain possession of such baggage until the amount, so due for boarding, lodging or rent, or either is paid; *provided*, that the provisions of this section shall not apply to stolen stock.

SEC. 2. Every common carrier of goods or passengers who shall, at the request of the owner of any personal goods, carry, convey or transport the same from one place to another; and any warehousemen or other person, who shall safely keep or store any personal property, at the request of the owner, or person lawfully in possession thereof, shall, in like manner, have a lien upon all such personal property, for his reasonable charges for the transportation, storage or keeping thereof, and for all reasonable and proper advances made thereon by him, in accordance with the usage and custom of common carriers and warehousemen.

Lien given to common carriers and warehousemen.

SEC. 3. Any mechanic or other person who shall make, alter, repair or bestow labor upon any article of personal property, for the improvement thereof, at the request of the owner of such personal property or of the materials from which the same is made, shall, in like manner, have a lien upon such articles of personal property for his reasonable charges for the labor performed and materials furnished and used in such making, alteration, repair or improvement.

Lien given to mechanics and laborers.

SEC. 4. If any such charges for which a lien is given by the three preceding sections, be not paid within thirty days after the same become due and payable, the mechanic, inn keeper, agistor, or other person to whom such lien is given as aforesaid, may apply to any Justice of the Peace of the county wherein he resides, to appoint appraisers to appraise the several articles of personal property whereon such lien is claimed. Such Justice shall thereupon appoint, by warrant under his hand and seal, three reputable householders of the county, not interested in the matter, to appraise such personal property.

Justice to appoint appraisers.

SEC. 5. The appraisers so appointed, shall be sworn by the Justice, to well and faithfully appraise and value all such personal property, and shall thereupon proceed to view and appraise the same, and shall return their appraisement, wherein shall be set down each article separately, to the Justice by whom they were appointed, within ten days after their appointment.

SEC. 6. After such appraisement is made, the person to whom such lien is given by the foregoing sections, may, after giving ten day's prior notice of the time, place and terms of such sale, with a description of the property to be sold, by publication in some newspaper published in the county wherein he resides, [or if there be no such newspaper, then by posting in three public places within such county], and delivering to the owner of such personal property, or if he do not reside in the county, transmitting by mail to him at his usual place of abode, if known, a copy of such notice, proceed to sell all such personal property, or so much thereof as may be necessary, at public auction, for cash in hand, at any public place within such county, between the hours of ten A. M. and four P. M. of the day appointed, and from the proceeds thereof, may pay the reasonable costs of such appraisement, notice and sale, aud his reasonable charges for which he has his lien, together with the reasonable cost of keeping such property up to the time of sale, the residue of the proceeds and of the property unsold, he shall render to the owner.

SEC. 7. No such sale shall be made for less than two-thirds of the appraised value of the article sold, nor except upon due notice, as required by the preceding section ; every such sale made in violation of the provisions of this section shall be absolutely void.

SEC. 8. At such sale, the person to whom such lien is given, may become the purchaser.

SEC. 9. In any case where the property to be sold cannot conveniently be sold in one day, the sale may be continued from day to day, by public outcry at the place of sale. Upon the completion of such sale, the person to whom the lien is given hereby, shall cause a sale bill thereof to be filed with the Justice of the Peace, before whom such appraisement was had, in which shall be set down the sum for which each separate article of property was sold, and the name of the purchaser. The Justice shall record such sale bill in his docket, and preserve the original thereof, together with the appraisement.

SEC. 10. Nothing herein shall be so construed as to take away the right of action of the party to whom such lien is given, for his charges, or for any residue thereof, after sale of such property.

SEC. 11. At such sale, the person to whom such lien is given, as herein provided, may appoint a clerk and crier.

SEC. 12. Appraisers appointed under the provisions of this act, shall receive one dollar per day; Justices of the Peace shall receive for each warrant of appraisement, fifty cents; for receiving and recording each appraisement, twenty cents for one hundred words, and the like fees for recording each sale bill; clerks and criers at sales made under the provisions hereof, shall receive each one dollar per day. *Compensation of appraisers and Justices.*

SEC. 13. Nothing in this act contained, shall be so construed as to affect any lien which may exist at the time this act shall take effect, or to take away the right or remedy to enforce the same, or to affect any right or remedy which may exist under and by virtue of any law which may be held to be repealed by this act, but as to all such liens or rights, the same shall remain in full force, and may be enforced in the same manner and to the same effect, as if this act had not been passed. *Saving clause.*

SEC. 14. Inasmuch as grave doubts exist as to whether any lien is now given upon personal property, an emergency exists, therefore, this act shall take effect from and after its passage. *Emergency clause.*

Approved February 12, 1883.

An Act to Amend Section One [1] of an Act for the Protection of Growing Crops. Approved February 12, 1881.

Justices to notify stock owners to keep stock in care of herders. SECTION 1. Section one of said act is hereby amended so as to read as follows: That the Justices of the Peace of the counties of Huerfano, Costilla, Conejos and Las Animas, in their respective precincts, are authorized and it is hereby made their duty to notify and require the inhabitants of their respective precincts, by public notice posted in not less than three public places in their respective precincts, on or before the twentieth day of April in each year, to keep in care of herders, all horses, mules, asses, neat cattle, hogs, sheep and goats, from the first day of May until the last day of October in each year.

Emergency clause. SEC. 2. It appearing to the General Assembly that on account of the near approach of the season for planting, an emergency exists, requiring the immediate taking effect of this act. It is therefore enacted that this act shall take effect and be in force from and after its passage.

Approved February 12, 1883.

Act approved February 12, 1881.

[See Laws of 1881, page 251.]

Damage by animals; when and how recovered. SEC. 4. In case of any damage done to planted trees by domestic animals, the owner of said trees may recover full damage from the owner of said animals, as provided in the last preceding section of this act; *provided*, said trees are planted inside of a lawful fence, or boxed to a height of not less than five feet.

———

[See Laws of 1879, page 190.]

An Act to Provide for the Herding of Rams.

SECTION 1. It shall be the duty of any owner, or agent of any owners of thoroughbred ram or rams of any description to herd them, or keep them enclosed. Any owner or agent who refuses to comply with the provisions of this act, shall be fined not less than twenty-five dollars nor more than one hundred dollars.

SEC. 2. Any fines arising from a violation of section one of this act, shall be paid into the school fund of the county in which such violation occurs.

Approved February 6, 1879.

[See Laws of 1879, page 190.]

AN ACT ENTITLED 'STALLIONS, JACKS, BULLS, RAMS AND BOARS.

SECTION 1. That the keepers of stallions, jacks, bulls, rams and boars, in this State, shall have liens upon the get of such for the space of one year from the birth of same, for the payment of service of such stallion, jack, bull, ram or boar.

SEC. 2. This act shall not apply to a *bona fide* purchaser without notice of such lien.

Approved January 31, 1879.

[See Laws of 1879, page 191.]

AN ACT TO PROTECT CATTLE FROM DISEASE CALLED TEXAS FEVER.

SECTION 1. No person or persons shall be allowed to drive any cattle into this State from the State of Texas or Indian Territory within six months next preceding, at any time after the first day of May and before the first day of September of any year; *provided*, that the provisions of this act shall not apply to persons driving or transporting such cattle on the usual routes of travel through the State expeditiously and without unnecessary delay. *Limitation of time for driving Texas cattle.*

SEC. 2. Any person violating the provisions of the first section of this act shall be guilty of a misdemeanor, and on conviction, shall be fined in any sum not less than one thousand dollars nor more than three thousand dollars. *Penalty for violation of section one.*

Approved February 12, 1879.

To Amend an Act Entitled "An Act Regulating the Branding, Herding and Care of Stock."

[Laws of 1874, page 252.]

SECTION 1. That any person or persons owning twenty-five [25] or more cows, shall not be allowed to let them run at large without providing and letting run at large with them, not less than one [1] bull, of good American graded stock, for each and every twenty-five [25] cows so owned and let run at large; and every person or persons who shall violate the provisions of this section, upon conviction in any court of this Territory, shall be fined in a sum not less than twenty-five [$25.00] nor more than two hundred dollars for each offense; *provided,* that this act shall apply only to the counties of Bent, El Paso, Pueblo and Elbert.

Approved February 13, 1874.

R. S. Chapter XCIII.—Sheep.

An Act to Provide for the Appointment of Sheep Inspectors.

[Session Laws, 1872.]

SECTION 1. The County Commissioners shall appoint a Sheep Inspector, who shall be a citizen of the county for which he is appointed, for each county containing two thousand sheep, who shall hold his office for two years, unless sooner removed; and any inspector may act in an adjoining county having no inspector, on request of the Commissioner thereof.

Appointment and term of office.

SEC. 2. It shall be the duty of the Sheep Inspector, whenever he has knowledge or information that any sheep within his jurisdiction have the scab or any other malignant contagious disease, to inspect said flock and report in writing the result of his inspection to the County Clerk of his county, to be filed by him for reference for the County Commissioners, or any party concerned; and if so dis-

[Session Laws 1879, page 184, sec. 1.]

Duties of sheep inspector.

eased, once every two weeks thereafter to reinspect said flock and report in writing the result and treatment, if any, in the same manner, until said disease is reported cured; *provided*, that in case of the removal of the flock six miles from the range of any other sheep, as hereinafter provided, he shall only make one inspection every three months. [Session Laws, 1877, page 185, sec. 2.]

SEC. 3. And upon the arrival of any flock of sheep into the State, the owner or agent shall immediately report them to the Inspector of the county for inspection, and the Inspector shall inspect and report as provided in section two ; and in case of failure, from any cause, of owner or agent, to report for inspection, a fine of one hundred dollars shall be imposed on said owner or agent for each offense, by any court of competent jurisdiction, which fine, when collected, shall be paid into the county treasury for the use of the Sheep Inspector's fund ; and any judgment for such fine shall be a lien upon such flock. *Report to inspector of arrival of stock in state; inspection in case of failure to report.*

SEC. 4. The owner or his agent of any flock reported by the Inspector to be so diseased shall immediately herd them, so that they cannot range upon or within one mile of any grounds accustomed to be ranged upon by any other sheep, and shall restrain them from passing over or traveling upon or within one mile of any public highway or road, and in case this cannot be done he shall immediately remove said sheep to a locality where they shall not be permitted to range within less than six miles of any other flock of sheep, and said sheep shall continue to be herded under the above restrictions until, upon inspection, they shall be reported free from such disease. *Duties of owner or agent of diseased flock.*

SEC. 5. The owner or his agent or employes of any flock of sheep, requiring or about to be inspected, shall afford the Inspector all reasonable facilities for making his inspection ; and for every violation of any of the provisions of this act said owner or his agent or his employes shall be fined not less than ten dollars, nor more than three hundred dollar, and every separate days offense shall *Penalty for violation of this act.*

constitute a separate offense, and the written report of an offense, made by an Inspector under oath, shall be *prima facie* evidence of the commission of said offense, and any Justice of the Peace of the county in which the offense is committed shall have jurisdiction thereof, and the Inspector shall *ex-officio* report all violations of the provisions of this act of which he has knowledge.

Oath and bond of inspector.

SEC. 6. Every Inspector before entering upon the duties of his office shall take the oath of office prescribed by law, and shall give bond to the State of Colorado in the sum of one thousand dollars, with good sureties, conditioned that he will faithfully perform the duties of his office ; such bond shall be approved by the County Clerk, who shall endorse upon every bond he shall approve as follows : " I am acquainted with the sureties herein, and believe them to be worth the amount of the sum of the within bond, over and above their just debts and liabilities."

Record of, and suits upon bond.

SEC. 7. Such bond, with the oath endorsed thereon, shall be recorded in the office of the Register of Deeds for the county in which the Inspector shall reside, and may be sued on by any person injured on account of the unfaithful performance of said Inspector's duties ; *provided*, that no suit shall be so instituted after more than twelve months have elapsed from the time the cause of action occurred.

Record of official act of inspector

SEC. 8. Every Inspector shall keep a fair and correct record of all his official acts, and, if required, give a certified copy of any record, upon payment of the fees therefor, and in case of the Inspector's death, resignation or removal, said record shall be deposited with the Register of Deeds.

[See sec. 3, Laws 1879, page 185.]

Fees of inspection.

SEC. 9. The Inspector shall receive for his services four dollars per day whilst necessarily employed in inspecting ; and for the first inspection an additional fee of one-half cent for every sheep, when the flock inspected is five hundred or less, and for inspecting larger flocks two dollars and fifty cents for the first five hundred, and one-fourth cent each for the remainder of said flock, to be paid by the owner or his agent, and two cents per line of ten words for any official report or document; *provided*, if any person shall keep several separate flocks of sheep, and some flock or flocks be not infected with scab, the owner shall be required to pay only the fees for inspection of such infected flock or flocks; [and] *provided* [*further*], that when an inspection is made, and the result shall show no disease, the Inspector shall give the owner a written statement to that effect, and shall be paid for said inspection as provided in section fifteen. The Inspector shall receive ten per cent. of all fines and penalties in cases in which he gives information of the offense, and his interest in the result shall not affect his competency as a witness, and all fines and penalties, except as herein provided, shall be paid to the County Treasurer as part of the sheep inspection fund of the county.

Disposition of fines and penalties.

SEC. 10. The notices herein shall be served by the Inspector, or the sheriff, or any constable of the county.

By whom notices to be served.

SEC. 11. That the counties of Las Animas, Huerfano, Costilla and Conejos are hereby excepted from the provisions of this act.

What counties excepted.

SEC. 12. Whenever a Sheep Inspector shall wilfully and falsely report any sheep subject to disease, he shall be subjected to a fine of ten times the amount of the fees charged by him for the inspection, and if he shall wilfully and falsely report any sheep inspected by him free from disease, that are thus infected, he shall be subjected to a penalty not exceeding three hundred dollars for each offense.

[See sec. 5, Laws 1879, page 186.]

Amount for false report by inspectors.

SEC. 13. If any Sheep Inspector shall be found guilty of either of the offenses set forth in section twelve, or if on complaint in writing by any three wool growers of the county, the County Commissioners, after allowing the Inspector a fair hearing, shall be of opinion that he is incompetent to discharge intelligently and efficiently the duties of his office, or that having sufficient knowledge or information he has for any cause wilfully or negligently

For what causes inspectors may be removed.

failed to make the required inspection, or that he has need-
lessly made inspections for the purpose of securing fees, or
that his reports have been influenced by favor or prejudice,
or from any cause he has failed in the proper discharge of
the duties of his office, it shall be the duty of said Commissioners to declare said Inspector's office vacant and to
make a new appointment.

Owner to dip on own premises; proviso. SEC. 14. That every owner of sheep having scab or
other malignant contagious disease shall dip or otherwise
treat the same upon his own premises; *provided*, that when
he has more than one ranch or set of ranches, and the diseased sheep are not upon the ranch where his dipping
works or other facilities for treating the disease are situated,
he shall have the right to drive through intermediate
ranges, but in so doing shall consult the owner's or occu-
pants of said range as to where he shall cross the same,
and in no case shall he enter another's corral, or water at
his troughs or accustomed watering place with his diseased sheep without the written or otherwise expressed
consent of the owner; and for every violation of the provisions herein he shall be subject to a penalty of not exceeding one hundred dollars.

Sheep inspectors fund; what shall constitute, how expended, etc. SEC. 15. That in each county there shall be levied
and assessed annually a tax not exceeding in any one year,
one-half of a mill upon the dollar of the assessed valuation
of the sheep within the county, which shall be collected as
other general taxes, and which, with the penalties herein
provided, shall constitute a sheep inspector's fund of the
county, and which fund shall only be expended in the payment of the legal fees of the Sheep Inspector, and said fees
shall only be paid by the County Treasurer after they shall
have been approved and allowed by the County Commissioners, in the same manner and form as claims against the
county are approved and allowed by them; and from said
fund the Sheep Inspector shall be paid not to exceed three
dollars per day for every day actually employed in making
his annual round between the tenth of August and the

tenth of December of each year, and three dollars per day for each day actually employed in making the inspection required by section [sections] two and three, and when he reports in substance no disease; *provided*, this act shall not affect or repeal section eleven of the act which this act is amendatory.

AN ACT TO PROHIBIT THE HERDING OF SHEEP IN THE NEIGHBORHOOD OF CITIES AND TOWNS, AND TO REPEAL ALL ACTS IN RELATION THERETO.

[R. S., page 844.]

SECTION 1. No person shall keep or herd sheep to the number of ten [10] or more at or within two [2] miles of any city, town or village in this State; *provided*, this act shall not prevent any one from driving sheep to market or from passing through any city town or village, with such animals, or from keeping the same in any enclosure, or from herding for threshing purposes in any city, town or village; *provided, further*, that this act shall not apply to any person who owns a stock ranch or farm within the above described limits.

At what distance from city, town or village sheep to be herded.

SEC. 2. Whoever shall offend against the prohibitions of this act shall pay a fine of twenty-five dollars for each day in which the offense may be continued, and such fine may be recovered by action of debt in the name of the people, before a Justice of the Peace or in the District Court of the proper county.

All acts and parts of acts in conflict with this act are hereby repealed.

Approved March 7, 1877.